For Naomi –
WARMLY,

Janice Rubin

Leah Lax

The Mikvah Project

Janice Rubin, Photographer

Leah Lax, Writer

Designed by Charles Wiese

Library of Congress Control Number 2001119128

ISBN: 0-9714909-0-2

Catalog and exhibition designed by Charles Wiese.

Printed in Houston, Texas by Wall Printing.

www.MikvahProject.com
P.O. Box 30298
Houston, TX 77249

The Mikvah Project exhibition and catalog were made possible
in part through the generous support of:

The Brown Foundation

The Nathan Cummings Foundation

Houston Endowment, Inc.

Joan Morgenstern

Texas Council For the Humanities

The Dobkin Family Foundation

Hadassah International Research Institute for Jewish Women

The Shefa Fund

Cultural Arts Council of Houston/Harris County

Harris and Eliza Kempner Fund

and

Mr. and Mrs. Bernard Appel

Gay Block and Malka Drucker

Carol Silverman Johnston

Jim and Sherry Kempner

Robert and Susan Lynch

Donna Gray Norquist

Sherwin Rubin

The Samuels Foundation

Patsy Williamson

and other generous contributors.

The Mikvah Project was created under the sponsorship of
the Jewish Community Center of Houston, and Women and Their Work of Austin, Texas

Acknowledgements

The making of the Mikvah Project became a significant personal journey for both of us. There are many people who helped along the way. First and foremost, we would like to thank Charles Wiese, who offered endless support and countless hours of editing of both photographs and text and whose sense of the sublime in his design contributed to every component of the project.

We are indebted to the women who agreed to model for the photographs. The Mikvah Project would not have been possible without their willingness and excitement for the project. Our sincere thanks go to Joann Fleischhauer, Karey Rawitcher, Kirsten Miles, Nina Rubin, Melissa Noble, Linda Ross, Galeet Dardashti, Rebecca Lowe, Rene Teague, Tamarie Cooper, Leslie Barnard, Julia Parmentier, and Robbi Sherwin.

Very special thanks and appreciation go to Charlotte Goldberg who was ready to drop whatever she was doing and cheerfully wade into the mikvah to lift up photo lights over her head while using her foot to hold Janice under the water. Additional photo assistance was provided by Tammy Krause who stood in the cold waters of the Blanco River, retaining a sense of humor that warmed us as our teeth chattered from the icy river.

The stories that women shared with us about their relationship to mikvah were often so intimate that we sometimes referred to our work as the "Mikvah Monologues" (after Eve Ensler's popular play). We recognize the courage it took for some women to trust us with their thoughts on this most private matter, and we are grateful for that trust. Their voices provide a personal, emotional component that gives the work its resonance.

We would like especially to acknowledge Joan Morgenstern who kept us going from the earliest stages of the project with her enthusiasm and her outstanding generosity. Jerry Wische, Executive Vice President of the Jewish Community Center of Houston believed in the value of our project, and together with Cultural Arts Director Marilyn Hassid, provided sponsorship and guidance. Chris Cowden, director of Women and Their Work in Austin, was also instrumental in the WATW sponsorship.

Financial support for our research and for the exhibition came through the assistance of several foundations and generous private individuals. We appreciate the broadminded vision of those who believed in the value of our work and chose to support it. Our deep gratitude goes to Sonia Simon Cummings of the Nathan Cummings Foundation, Emily Todd at the Houston Endowment, and to Jennifer McClung of the Texas Council for The Humanities for their continued interest in the project.

In the course of our work, we have received the aid and guidance of many friends. Sandy Sheehy helped nurture the original possibility of the expanded exploration and traveling exhibition. Mary Winkler, Clint Willour, Rabbi Judith Abrams, Bronya Shaffer, Marv Hoffman, and Rosellen Brown each served in an advisory capacity, and as a sounding board for ideas. Several more people offered useful critiques and advice and helped us put the work in perspective: Jean Caslin, Lloyd Wolf, Sharon Stewart, Judy Goldman, Sandi Dubowski, Ellen Orseck, Rachel Davis, Theodora De Francesco, Karen Bering, and Barbara Loeser. Rachel Adler's outstanding scholarship and interest in our project provided invaluable perspective for Leah's critical essays. Ann McCutcheon, David Theis, and Cynthia Freeland provided additional editorial advice for the catalog essays.

There are countless others who helped bring this project to life. Ken Knezick helped in the realization of Janice's vision of underwater photography by providing generous technical support and equipment. Mike Hefner, Jeff Myers, Marci DeBock, and Jamie Powers each provided access to equipment and technical advice. The staff at the Drisha Institute in New York became an unexpected and valuable resource. Many thanks to those who opened their homes to us as we traveled across the country conducting interviews for this project. We are grateful to Rabbi and Rebbetzin Shimon Lazaroff and Rabbi Joseph Radinsky as well as to Camp Young Judea Texas for allowing access to their facilities to make photographs for this project. We appreciate their trust that this subject would be treated with dignity and respect.

We would like to thank our friends, family, and our children and especially our husbands for their patience and for their love and support. And finally, we turn to one another with deepest thanks in appreciation of friendship, mutual inspiration, and the shared creative collaboration that has made this quite a journey.

Janice Rubin and Leah Lax
November, 2001

Beneath the Surface

by Janice Rubin

As a child, I remember sneaking into the back room of the synagogue to marvel at the mikvah, a great, green tiled tub that was bigger and deeper than me. My mother told me that brides bathed there. Until I began exploring Mikvah for this project, I had little interest in what I considered to be an archaic custom. I had scoffed at the ritual, which seemed to perpetuate the religious myth that women in general, and menstruating women in particular, were "unclean." But all of that is based on a misinterpretation of the mysterious biblical word *tahmeh*, which has no equivalent in English. Several of my life experiences – marriage, years of aching to be a parent, the transcendent birth of my own child, and watching from my grandfather's bedside as his soul left this world – led me to interpret the word *tahmeh* to mean "spiritually vulnerable."

I became interested in exploring the mikvah when I was feeling stifled by several things in my life. I felt stuck in my career and I wanted to explore new ways of seeing with my camera. I needed to improve the connections in my personal relationships. I read Leah Lax's story about a mikvah attendant and started thinking about immersion in a mikvah as an opportunity for emotional cleansing and spiritual transformation, for personal movement and growth. I knew that I had to have the experience myself before I started to photograph. Descending the narrow steps on my first trip into the tiled pool, I was conscious of a heightening of my senses. Under the water, sound and space seemed distorted and expanded, as the light danced and shimmered beneath the surface of the water.

During my twenty-five years as a photographer, I have used my camera to make images in moonlight and daylight, and from helicopters, horseback, even dangling from a tall sailing ship. My challenge has always been to find the juxtaposition of light and subject that would evoke an emotional response. Before I began this project I had never photographed underwater; the experience provided exciting new possibilities. It was fascinating to discover what a woman looked like photographed in the small, warm, sensuous space of the mikvah.

Although I wanted to capture the actual experience of this ritual on film, I chose to photograph models in simulated immersions out of respect for the modesty that is an integral component in the lives of mikvah-observant women. My intent was to create images that evoke the ritual rather than create a true-life visual record that would have betrayed the privacy of the individual. Later, when Leah and I began to interview women about their actual experiences, we took care to protect their identities.

Some of the most successful images depended on the mindset, the sensibility of the model. I tried to find women who were at a place of transition in their lives. As I worked, I felt a personal connection with the women, past and present, who have maintained this ancient ritual. When I was in the water, I tried to imagine all of the women who came before me. What was the mikvah like in the small Jewish villages of Eastern Europe where my great-grandmothers carried on the tradition of their mothers?

The first exhibit of my immersion photographs was held at Diverse Works in Houston in March, 2000. It was then that women began to approach me and whisper their own mikvah stories. It wasn't long before I realized that mikvah was making a comeback, and that the ritual was also being reinvented in ways I'd never imagined. Subsequent to that, I asked Leah to join me on what became an inspiring journey to document some of the intimate, personal stories of women speaking about their relationship to this ritual and the role it plays in their lives.

The photographs and interviews in this exhibition do not attempt to tell the full story of mikvah practice in America. They represent a small sample of women from across the country who are using this ancient ritual, both in traditional and innovative ways. We spoke to Jewish women from every denominational background – from Chassidic to unaffiliated.

My goal was to create a faceless portrait that would resonate with each woman's story and accompany her interview. This led me to define my work within both cultural and visual constraints. While photographing underwater, I struggled to make photographs that would retain a sense of mystery while respecting the modesty inherent in the ritual. Creating the faceless portraits allowed me to become a visual storyteller, portraying something unique to each subject, a window into her life.

I have been asked how I managed to hold my breath long enough to make these images underwater. In fact, sitting on the bottom of the small pool watching an immersion felt like a kind of meditation. I realized only afterward that I always hold my breath when I photograph. It was as if the act of photographing sustained me.

It is my hope that this work will resonate, not only for Jewish women, but for women from different backgrounds as well. In the course of this project, women from other traditions have approached me to describe water immersion rituals in their own cultures. I feel that the project has the potential to broaden understanding between cultures by focusing on our common relationship with one of life's most essential substances – water.

MIKVAH: An ancient ritual bath in which Jewish women traditionally immerse after their monthly cycle and before the resumption of sexual relations. Also used for conversion.

MIKVAH: Passed down from mother to daughter for over three thousand years, it is a thoroughly private, even secret practice. Today it is a many-faceted silent celebration of womanhood observed across a broad spectrum of Jewish women.

The Mikvah in History

by Leah Lax

The small, tiled pool is filled with warm water to shoulder height. A woman stands alone, poised on the steps leading into this ritual bath that Jewish women have been using for millennia. Under the five-foot-square pool hides one more container that collects "living water" from a natural source. Through a conduit, this water "kisses" the filtered, chlorinated water in the immersion pool.

The woman descends the steps and slowly sinks beneath the surface with knees pulled up and arms outward, submerged in the water, in herself, in God. Then she stands, covers her head with a cloth, crosses her arms over her bare chest, and recites the ancient prescribed blessing. Again she slips beneath the water. For a moment she is poised there as if the water can sustain her. And then she emerges, fresh and sensual and real.

The secret practice of mikvah immersion has been a powerful, silent presence in the history of Jewish life. The *Shulchan Aruch*, the centuries-old source book of Jewish law, states that if a group of Jews wants to establish a new community and funds are limited, building a mikvah is to take priority over the purchase of a Torah scroll. These pools can be found in closed rooms in the backs of synagogues or in unobtrusive, free-standing buildings. Historically, mikvah has been viewed as the guardian of the sanctity of marriage and the purity of the souls of the children born to that marriage. The Torah scroll was the source of daily Jewish identity and clarified the boundaries of the Jewish community. But the mikvah gave the community a future. Without a future, the daily laws were useless, which is why the mikvah was to precede even the scroll of the Law.

The position of honor once held for mikvah in the Jewish community at large is rooted in that Torah scroll. Chapter Fifteen in Leviticus presents a woman as just another in a list of those who must separate from the community after an "emission," or for a woman after her menses, until he or she is cleansed and immerses in a mikvah. The requirement of immersion is one of the ancient purity laws that guaranteed the level of spiritual cleanliness necessary before entering the Temple or presenting a sacrifice. Immersion was also required after contact with the dead.

Chapter Eighteen in Leviticus gives an example of the holiness laws. These were laws that legislated specific values and modes of conduct and dress that were to be unique to the Jewish nation. It is here that we find a stringent warning. If a man has sexual relations with a "niddah," a menstruating woman who has not yet been to the mikvah, he will be spiritually cut off from the Jewish people. This is part of a general message: if Jews do not define themselves as different, then they will be absorbed into the surrounding cultures and lose their identity as Jews. After the destruction of the Temple and dispersal of the Jews by the Romans in 70 CE, the purity laws were no longer relevant, but the code of holiness became a means of preserving identity. And the injunction against sexual relations before mikvah is among these laws.

This is why Jewish women continued to be required to immerse themselves in a mikvah after the destruction of the Temple, and why women's immersion has always carried with it a kind of urgency that has led to startling stories of courage and self-sacrifice for mikvah. A body of humane and detailed laws and guidelines governing sexual behavior, all seeking to elevate the sexual act, preserve its modesty, and protect the woman, grew around the laws of mikvah immersion. Jewish law specifies that immersion is to continue once each month seven days after the conclusion of the menses. From the beginning of the cycle until the mikvah immersion, the husband and wife are to have no physical contact. The mikvah immersion is intended to be a herald to the resumption of sexual relations. Mikvah also became the introduction to marriage, to be performed by the bride for the first time on the night before the wedding. The intimacy of this nude immersion that leads to the woman's return to her husband resulted in a culture of secrecy and modesty surrounding this observance, which has always been performed under cloak of night and not disclosed to anyone.

Over centuries, a variety of attitudes arose affecting cultural behavior in relation to mikvah. Negative superstitions about a woman who was a "niddah" contributed to the marginalizing of women in Jewish life. There are many comments in Jewish texts reinforcing such attitudes.

A custom of immersion for men as a personal preparation for prayer has also continued until modern times, although men's immersion is not technically required by Jewish law. Many Jewish men have maintained a family legacy of ritual immersion before the Sabbath and holidays. Unlike the women, men will immerse in small groups of family or community members, and often value the sharing of this private ritual and the deep sense of group spirituality. Along with the recent resurgence and reclaiming of mikvah among Jewish women, there has been a parallel renewed interest in mikvah among Jewish men.

The Orthodox presentation of mikvah has changed radically in recent years along with a greater sensitivity to feminist consciousness. The change in presentation is very unusual in a community that seeks to remain relatively static in philosophy and practice. Popular books from Orthodox sources now emphasize traditional mikvah observance as respectful of women's boundaries, encouraging better communication between partners, and as an erotic enhancement to the marital relationship. The period of separation is presented as one that fosters desire and leads to a monthly renewal in the marriage.

The fresh approach has allowed a new generation of mikvah observant women greater comfort in the context of mikvah. Perhaps this change within the Orthodox community prepared the way for the more recent interest in mikvah immersion in the Jewish community at large.

Today, there has been a rejuvenation of mikvah observance that crosses denominational lines within Judaism. Community mikvahs are being built to accommodate all types of Jewish congregations, and many longstanding mikvahs have been renovated to satisfy new demand. Immersion has been expanded to apply to personal needs, functioning, for instance, as a life transition marker or a means of healing from trauma. The ritual of immersion in its resurgence is a powerful tool in the modern search for spirituality and meaning. Its ancient components link water and the female body in ways that evoke images of birth and creation. Mikvah becomes a meditation on the spiritual and its mystery.

Out of the Silence

by Leah Lax

In December of 1999 I gave my friend, Janice Rubin, a copy of "Munya's Story," my short story about a mikvah attendant who confronts a survivor of sexual abuse. In it, the survivor seeks to use the ritual of mikvah as a tool for healing. Janice became intrigued by the idea that women were stretching the parameters of traditional mikvah use for all kinds of personal needs. We spent one entire evening until the early hours brainstorming possibilities of mikvah and photography.

The plan at first was to simulate immersions and photograph models in the mikvah from beneath the water surface. It seemed that the mikvah water might evoke in the models a sense of transition to a new place, or a feeling of embrace. I never verbalized these things to Janice. I came to see the act of photography as wordless and intuitive. I watched, and sometimes waded in and held the light equipment, as Janice sat under the water at the bottom of the mikvah with a waterproof camera, wearing goggles and weights on her wrists. Her image shimmered beneath the surface as a kind of underwater magic unfolded. I saw before me a swirl of primal elements: the female body, ancient water, whispers of birth, death, rejuvenation, transcendence.

Janice had caught the mystery and the very private, raw blending of the feminine physical self with spirituality. To me, the figures captured on film in the act of immersion appeared inner-focused, in a new and private dimension.

I had been willing to facilitate Janice's photographic exploration of mikvah, but when she asked me to join her in an expanded project and conduct a series of interviews, I had to admit and explain my ambivalence. After years of lecturing on the topic, years in which I had accompanied hundreds of women to the mikvah as a personal mikvah attendant, I was moving away from my enthusiasm. I had struggled, and I had watched others struggle, with the demands the mikvah laws made on a marriage. Janice's invitation brought me in direct confrontation with my ambivalence. Perhaps, I finally decided, The Mikvah Project would be an exploration for both of us.

We began to collect interviews with women about their mikvah experiences. I was seeking to understand why mikvah seemed to touch women so deeply, and the more I heard, the more I wanted to explore a use that, in the context of some of the lives we encountered, was unexpected.

The earliest attempt that I know of to move mikvah out of the sole ownership of Orthodoxy and into the public realm was in 1974, when the Lubavitcher Rebbe, the leader of the Lubavitch Chassidic movement, spoke to a gathering of thousands and called for open education and dissemination of mikvah observance. The speech sent shock waves through the Orthodox community. The Lubavitcher's call was unprecedented, radical in that world, and met confusion, public opposition, or in many cases a kind of lip service that didn't do justice to the depth of the call. Mikvah observance is still considered by the Orthodox to be central to a Jewish home, the guarantor of propriety and holiness for the marriage and children. But that centrality doesn't give it public forum. The objections to the Rebbe's speech came from the conviction that mikvah, always a private affair, should remain steeped in its traditional modesty.

For generations Jewish women have gone to the mikvah in secret. The children in the mikvah-observant families often grow up uninformed of their mother's monthly practice. The gradual awareness on the part of these children, through clues and observations never verbalized, becomes part of a budding awareness that parallels their own unfolding sexuality. One of our subjects told us "As an adolescent, I began to notice that my mother left the house once a month with wet hair saying she was going to a meeting, and then she came back an hour and a half later with wet hair."

The Rebbe later asserted that, if the Orthodox and Chassidic communities didn't educate their members about the laws – and he meant the whole body of laws about Jewish sexuality that surround the practice of mikvah - their girls would acquire their education on such intimate matters from magazines. He was quite aware of the turn away from traditional values that such a secular "education" would effect.

Since that early effort by the Rebbe to disseminate information about mikvah openly, there has been a move toward mikvah observance beyond the bounds of the Orthodox community. In part, I think it comes from a reaction to the modern sense of being adrift, a desire for renewed connection to old values, and perhaps a search for spiritual depth in an un-spirited world. I was particularly intrigued with this new use. It generated an excitement among the more secular Jewish women, and I wanted to explore the new parameters they were giving this observance. Janice and I found mikvah being used in creative rituals for healing and for a variety of personal events such as life transitions.

But until this recent renewed interest, mikvah observance had waned in the twentieth century. There were many factors. An immigrant generation lacked the funds to build and maintain these ritual baths. There was a drift away from Jewish traditional observance as the new Jewish generation sought to Americanize and differentiate themselves from the old. As a result, Jewish education in general was not strong, and it did not include teachings about the mikvah laws. The emergent feminist movement sparked an attitude that the observance branded women as unclean. The division of the Jewish community into its current branches cut the majority off from awareness of the largely secretive practice of mikvah maintained in Orthodox communities.

In recent times, the traditional secrecy worked against survival of the rite. Daughters weren't learning about mikvah from their mothers until they faced marriage, after new societal attitudes had already taken hold. Brides looked aghast at those rabbis who still requested that they immerse in a mikvah before marriage. A whole generation of Jewish mothers defined mikvah to their daughters, if the subject ever came up, as an old-world and backward practice not attuned to their sanitized lives. I received a similar message from the previous generation in my family.

The prohibition against sexual relations with a woman who has not been to the mikvah that month is so strong, and mikvah has been deemed so essential to marriage, that it has resulted in modern day stories of women who risked their lives to perform their monthly immersions. "Mikvah," a Russian refugee told us, "was the only way that I could be married." For her, the yoke of Jewish law was total. Her sexuality could have no expression, and the Jewish people no future, without mikvah. I came to feel that people like her are the ones who have ensured the survival of this ancient ritual.

The Russian refugee told us of the illegal mikvah outside of Leningrad that she used when she was eighteen and a new bride. I felt I was there with her as she described her nude descent down the icy steps of a ladder, in pitch dark beneath someone's kitchen floor, to immerse in freezing water, knowing that, if anyone ever spoke about it, she'd end up in Siberia.

"I tried to put my foot in," she told us, "But I kept taking it out. My friend said, 'Go one time.' I said, 'I cannot.' Again I tried. Many times I put in a foot and pulled it out, suffered, but I went down the ladder. It had ice on it. Into the water. Very dark. Very, very cold. And I came out. Somehow I came out."

Janice and I interviewed women in New York, Chicago, Denver, Houston and Los Angeles. Although the vast majority of mikvah users are Orthodox, and the new interest in mikvah among other groups is relatively new and not large, our group of interviewees does not reflect that demographic. About half of our subjects were Orthodox women who observed mikvah and all of its attendant laws as part of an unchallenged adherence to Jewish law, and the other half were women who had adopted mikvah for other, personal reasons. We included women who had single experiences in a mikvah as part of a creative ritual.

There seemed to be a kind of raw confrontation that occurred in the waters. "In the mikvah," one of the women told us, "you are stripped of all pretense, all illusions. You can't hide; not from yourself and not from God." Some women told us they feel momentarily placed in another dimension during immersion. The mikvah is its own timeless space, at once both resonant with history and so private that it seems, in the moment, clean of connection to the world outside.

Immersion has long been the transition point that signaled a change in status, such as from non-Jew to Jew (in the conversion ritual), from unmarried to married, from *tameh,* a status that forbids sexual relations, to *tahor,* when sexual relations are permitted. Now it is being used for other transitions as well. "I needed something to divide that portion of my life from what was to come," a woman who was recently divorced told us. "From that point on I could look forward instead of backward."

Women talked about the primal sense in the mikvah, and compared its warm, clean water to fetal waters and the emergence to birth. Mikvah seems to have enormous potential as a way to an expanded, feminine and spiritual identity for contemporary women. Many spoke of the sense of rejuvenation, strengthening, and discovery of a spiritual core.

It was that sense of potential, and that quest for understanding the depth of the appeal, that led me to one home, among others, to probe the nature of a particular woman's mikvah observance. Like most of the women we interviewed, she had never spoken to anyone about her practice. There was a raw moment in the interview, one with tears, in which she asserted the sense of private, real confrontation with self and God; the "just me and God" moment that we often heard and which always moved us.

She talked about how pressured she felt in her early years by the sexual permissiveness of the era. Sex seemed to have become a currency. For her, the period of abstention before her mikvah immersion has become a declaration that no one has free license to her body. She also spoke about the eroticized female forms that bombard our culture and the personal pain with her own form that media-generated images have caused her. She felt that the nude confrontation with God in the mikvah was a most basic validation.

The mikvah laws seek to imbue the sexual act and the marital relationship as a whole with a kind of sanctity. "Mikvah entails monogamy," she told me. "It says that sex is holy and private. As a teen growing up in the sixties, no one I knew believed that way. I was going to move to New York, become a poet, and never let anybody hurt me."

Once again I was looking at a life through the lens of mikvah. This interview seemed to summarize themes that arose in many other interviews. I saw in it a host of modern, cultural struggles: with casual sex, with self comparison to idealized images in society, with self-ownership, the breakdown of monogamy, and the existential angst of desire for meaning. For this woman, mikvah was a tool to confront it all.

Although the immersion is traditionally the culmination of a period of abstention and completes a transition back to intimacy, I was surprised that the majority of the women did not talk about that aspect of mikvah. It seemed they had appropriated mikvah immersion away from issues related to the marital relationship, out of its original context, in a search for spirituality. Mikvah, for these women, had become a solitary, very feminine rite.

There were those who did talk about the impact of mikvah on the marital relationship. The period of abstention before mikvah immersion was a particular focus. "I treasure the intensity of longing for my husband during the separation period as part of going to mikvah," one woman told us. "It is frustrating, agonizing, wonderful." For her and others, that separation increased desire and strengthened the marital bond, and the monthly return to intimacy was a special joy that remained fresh. Over the last twenty years, a number of handbooks have been published touting mikvah observance as the guarantee of a monthly honeymoon. I found that this actually worked for some of our subjects. For others, the separation period was a strain.

It seemed to me that a new generation of mikvah observant women had greater comfort with their physical selves in the context of mikvah. It is a clearly contemporary phenomenon that a nineteen-year-old Chassidic bride was able to speak to us in as open a manner as she did, with an unabashed awareness of her sexuality. She described her immersion on the night before her wedding, of how she cried through the entire process.

"I thought I would have this amazing spiritual experience," she told us, "but I don't even know what that means. I cried the whole time, and I didn't know why I was crying. Sexuality hadn't entered my life yet, but I was going to the mikvah in order that it would. When I went in on the night before my wedding, I had this overwhelming sense that I was going in that water a girl, and coming out a woman."

Another young woman went to mikvah as part of her coming out as a lesbian. She hoped that her immersion would help her to deal with the negative impact of the revelation on her relationship with her parents. She said the immersion made her realize that "there was something larger than me working my life." When she emerged from the water, she found herself facing a freestanding, full-length mirror in an undeniable and timely assertion of her physical being. "Mikvah was a turning point for me in living with my sexuality. Coming from a Jewish tradition," she told us, "I don't see such a big division between spirit and physical, mind and body."

For some women, mikvah has moved past the sexual aspect to a more spiritual lesson in the body itself. One unmarried woman we interviewed goes to mikvah every month as a way of re-orienting herself, as a means of *tshuvah*, or of return to her Jewish values. Her preparations for immersion – the careful manicure, pedicure, and thorough body cleansing required before the ritual – become a form of prayer. As she removes her polish and files her nails, she asks herself questions. "These hands," she wonders. "What did they do in the past month? What and who did they reach out to? What opportunities did they allow to pass? What will I commit them to for the following month?" She continues in that vein with each part of her body as she scrubs it. I was quite moved by this account of her reverie in the bathtub.

Nevertheless, we found women who were unhappy with aspects of their mikvah observance. A few reported difficult experiences with mikvah attendants or with the waiting areas. In large, mikvah observant communities, the attendants are sometimes impatient. "I came to mikvah before my wedding," a woman told us, "with a deep feeling that something there is special, but I was alone, without family. The attendant said, 'You're not such a young bride, are you?' This wasn't the celebration I had wanted." One subject said to us, "I sensed there was something significant about mikvah that wasn't in those syrupy books people gave me; something primordial, something transcendent, but I just couldn't access it. I felt exposed sitting in that waiting room with the other women. And it reminded me too much of African menstrual huts."

Adherence to the laws governing the period of abstinence before immersion (a minimum of twelve days per month) can cause discomfort and defiance. When she was ten years old, one Orthodox subject discovered a book in her home that detailed the mikvah laws. "The part that shocked and disturbed me," she said, "was the discussion about the internal examinations you are supposed to make with a small cloth during the final seven days of the period of abstinence. I got really scared. I didn't feel comfortable going and asking anyone, 'What the heck is this about?' Instead, I said, 'I am not growing up.' I had a hard time, a lot of negative feelings, about my own sexuality through much of my adolescence."

Eventually her discomfort with the mikvah laws led her to a modern women's yeshiva, where she became a scholar in the Talmudic sections pertaining to mikvah. Married and mikvah observant today, she teaches at the same institution where she had gone to study, and her life's labor is invested in the struggle toward a reconciliation of the mikvah laws with her own needs, a reconciliation that she does not think is possible. Still, her life is that effort. Her classes are filled with women grateful for a place where they can meet openly, sharing honest and personal responses to controversial laws. Debate becomes heated. "I want to preserve the integrity of the mikvah laws," she told us, "*and* my own integrity, because both are articulations of who I am."

Despite ongoing discussion and contradictions, there is something about the nude entry into the mikvah water that demands self-honesty. One Orthodox woman from Jerusalem spoke to us of how she concealed her homosexuality through the years of her marriage and the birth of five children. She told us how she prayed each month in the mikvah that she would immerse "and come up straight." Then came the day when she immersed and did just that. "I came up straight – straight in my own head with who I am." She stood in the water and cried, and then went home, sat her five small children down in a row on the sofa, boys with yarmalkas and soft, curling sidelocks, girls in modest skirts and long sleeves, and she told them, "Mommy can only be married to a woman."

Particularly moving were the women who went to mikvah as a means of healing from or coping with trauma. One woman spoke of harrowing sexual abuse as a small child, and of how she came to mikvah to feel clean again, and to heal. "I stood in front of the water before my immersion," she said, "and I promised God that I would allow myself to be a woman." Another continued to go to the mikvah each month in the face of abject pain, and asserted that the regular immersions helped her through the ordeal. "During my illness," she told us, "I was this howling, hurt, trapped animal – a completely physical creature. And then, for the moment when my head slipped under the surface of the mikvah water, I became a spiritual person. I had escaped."

One of our last interviews, an elderly woman who went to mikvah the single time required by Jewish law after menopause, spoke about how mikvah helped her face death. "The way I felt when I went in the mikvah, I'm sure that in the womb that is how you feel, and we're probably going back there. It felt like home, after you die, and we'll feel at peace, without worry or anything. That is where we're going back, I'm sure."

In the course of conducting The Mikvah Project, Janice and I found quite a range of creative and personal applications of mikvah use. We were stunned by how rich and varied the ritual had become. Mikvah today has taken on a new shape, and I found myself excited because so much of what our subjects told us had not been heard before. Even the more secular Jewish women had fallen into the ancient mode of secrecy about mikvah immersion. I felt privileged that we were able to offer these women something they did not have before – an opportunity to speak about the central issues in their lives that the mikvah has touched. I saw each one of the women as a partner in our work to bring this ancient ritual out of the silence.

———————————

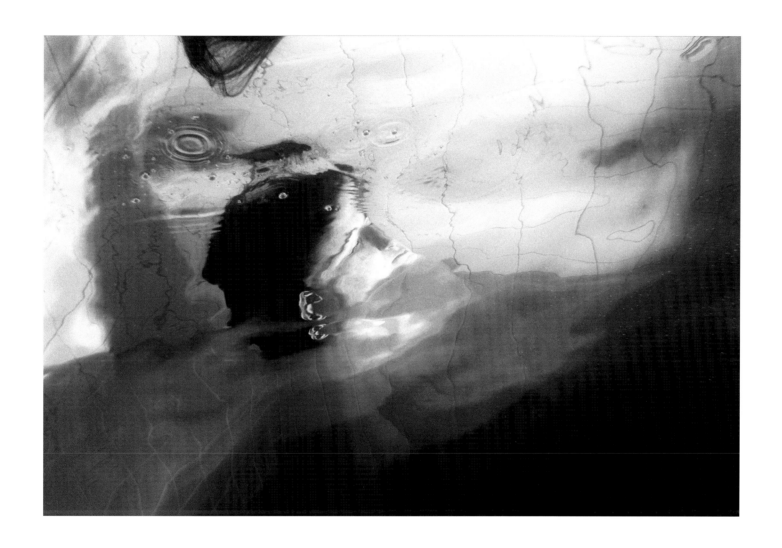

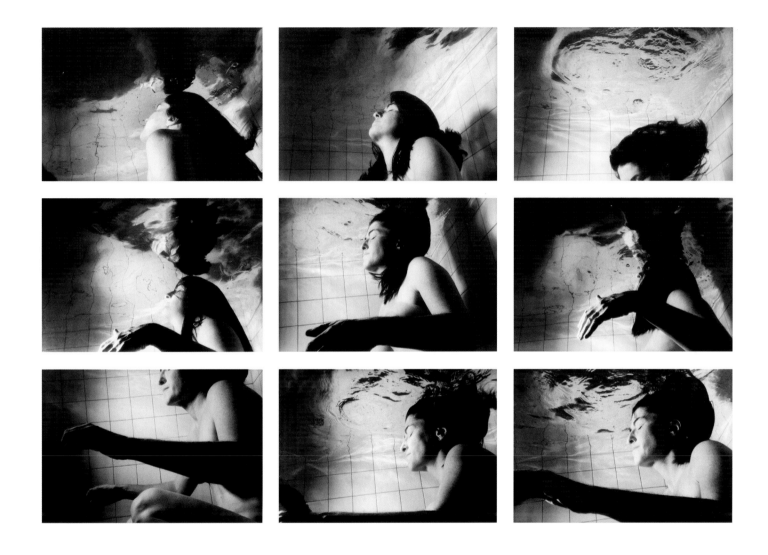

Those seven days of abstention before mikvah are a trial. When we first got married, we tried to follow the laws in every detail. Cold turkey. No touching during those seven days. I didn't even pass him a plate. He didn't kiss me or hold my hand.

I was so angry. Look, this was too fast, too soon. So we realized that for a while we had to make compromises. We decided we could only kiss and hug outside.

We were living in an apartment. Up on the roof we'd go. We couldn't be touching each other in the house. That would be too tempting.

I'm seventy-six years old. When I announced my recent engagement, one of my very best friends said, "I'm going to give you a mikvah party!" I looked at her and I said, "You must be insane." First of all, at my age, never having been to mikvah, why would I go now? I always thought that a woman goes after her period to be cleansed. I said, "Well, I don't need that. I take baths."

You know, I've always been a spiritual person inside, but mikvah has enforced that. The way I felt when I went to mikvah – I'm sure that in the womb that is how you feel, and we're probably going back there. It's like home, after you die, and we'll feel at peace, without worry or anything.

Sexuality hadn't entered my life yet, but I was going to the
mikvah in order that it would. When I went in on the night
before my wedding, I had this overwhelming feeling that
I'm going to come out of this mikvah a different person –
going in a girl and coming out a woman.

Before he died, my husband used to tell me that I was so special to him that he saw an aura around me. Just the touch of his hand radiated into my arms, and it came to my heart.

Once, during the period of separation, he said, "Let's ask the rabbi whether we can wear gloves and hold hands." So the first thing he always did after I went to the mikvah was touch my hand. And he told me, "You are so, so holy."

I knew that mikvah would not be the only thing I needed to help me heal from sexual abuse, but I still began to go every year before Yom Kippur. One time I remember leaving the mikvah and crying on the way home, saying it was all a lie. I'd been made to believe all these bad things about myself over the years, but God's truth was that I was clean.

I'm twenty-seven, and I came out to my family as a lesbian last January. Until that point I had a very close relationship with my parents, but that changed everything. It was a very painful experience. I decided to go to mikvah to help me heal.

Mikvah was a turning point for me in living with my sexuality. Coming from a Jewish tradition, I don't see such a big division between spirit and physical, mind and body.

I was in a physically abusive relationship. It took a year of going to the mikvah before I felt like whatever skin he touched wasn't there any more. Mikvah brought me back to myself.

Now, as I prepare myself for the mikvah, I think about the actions of different parts of my body since the last time I was there. These hands (I think while I'm doing my nails), who have I touched and not touched? And my eyes (and I might be removing my makeup), what did I see in people? What did I fail to see? And my feet (and I'd be doing a pedicure), where have my feet been? What did they run to do? It's sort of a private Yom Kippur.

My last immersion helped me heal. I was saying good-bye, not just to my uterus and ovaries, but to mikvah, and to whatever I had as a woman that was now gone. I didn't say any prayer beyond the traditional one. For me, mikvah was a wordless, wonderful thing.

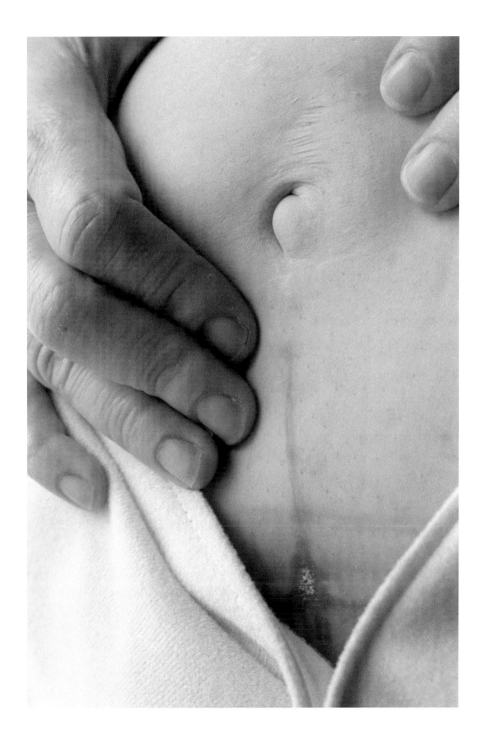

Through nine years of infertility, it was like a death memorial every time I got my period. And then, when I was ready to go to the mikvah each month, it was a restoration of hope. I'd had that time to mourn.

This is the man I love. I went through two horrendous marriages before I finally found the right guy. I want babies with him. I want clones of this man.

My first marriage was an arranged marriage when I was seventeen. Mikvah was something that I accepted in the same way we accepted other rules, even though I may not have liked them or understood why. When I married the second time, mikvah still meant nothing to me. Zero.

When I stood in the mikvah on the night before my third wedding, I started crying. Each time I went down I felt more engulfed by the water, more purified by the water. The immersion that was supposed to be a preparation for getting married became an act of being born. In that short time I made a commitment that this is something I'm going to observe for me. No one is making me do it.

When I prepare for mikvah, it's a family affair. In the Syrian Jewish community, we were taught that if you do this *mitzvah*, and do it right, you will have a good marriage and a good life, so everyone goes to mikvah, and they are very open about it.

I used to walk my mother to the mikvah when she went on the Sabbath or holidays. My mother and my grandmother made me feel I had this exciting, wonderful thing to look forward to. I'm going to tell my daughters how it feels to have that quiet time in the mikvah. I want them to know the special quality it gives a marriage.

I got married in 1939 in Odessa. I was seventeen years old. I had to go into the Black Sea to go to mikvah. My mother and sister went there every month, winter and summer, but I was afraid of the waves. I just couldn't do it, so my husband and I moved to Leningrad where there was a mikvah that the Soviets had not closed.

Later, the Soviets did close the Leningrad mikvah, but I found an old man with a secret mikvah he'd dug under his kitchen floor. It was winter, and the mikvah was completely dark, with icy, wooden steps and freezing water. Immersing in that was the hardest thing I've ever done, and we both knew that if either of us told anyone, we'd be sent to Siberia.

Mikvah observance entails monogamy. It says that sex is holy and private. As a teen in the sixties, no one I knew believed in those things. I was going to live alone, move to New York and be a poet, and never let anybody hurt me.

I left the church when I was sixteen. It just wasn't right for me, although there was good singing.

After I got approval for my conversion in Israel, the rabbis were very slow to give me the go-ahead for mikvah. So I called them every day. I told them how awful it was that they were making me live through another Sabbath before I could be a Jew. It turned out that was just what they wanted to hear.

For me, mikvah was always simply something that had to be done, it was the right time and you just went. I go to mikvah, and I help other women to go, but at this point, my feeling about it is that it's a chore. I look forward to menopause, when I will stop going to mikvah.

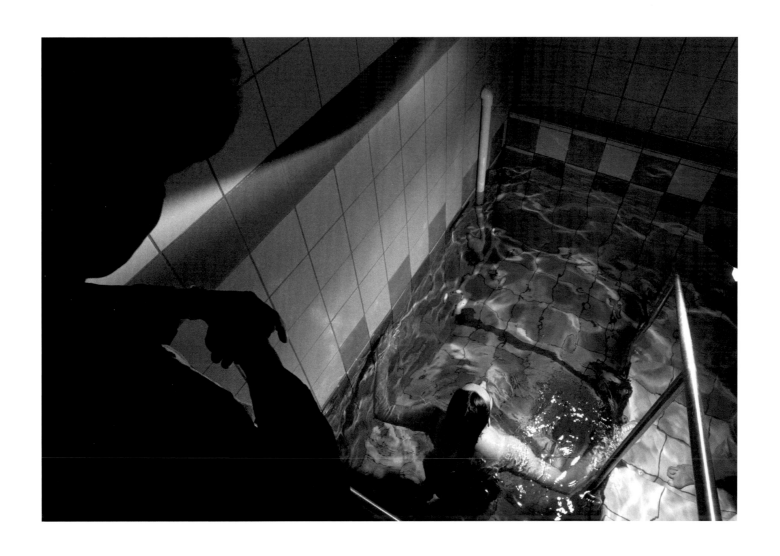

My ex-husband had moved out two years before, and I knew that the marriage was over. We had a Jewish divorce, but in my mind and in my heart I just couldn't let go of the marriage.

I thought mikvah could create a way to help me bridge this difficult period. Mikvah immersion left me feeling washed free of this overlay of guilt and "what if." From that night on I could look forward instead of backward.

My cousin took her sisters and her mother with her to the mikvah on the night before her wedding. They threw candies on the bride when she came out and they sang.

I came to mikvah before my wedding with a deep feeling that something there must be special. But I was alone, without family, and the attendant said to me, "You're not such a young bride, are you?" This wasn't the celebration I had wanted.

Part of the power and mystique of mikvah is that it's hidden. That's what gives it beauty. I think it's okay that my mother never told me about her mikvah observance, or that, growing up in an orthodox community, I knew so little about sexuality when I got married. There's something sweet about feeling awkward with your husband in the beginning. Then you grow together.

I treasure the longing for my husband during the separation period as part of going to mikvah. It is frustrating, agonizing, wonderful. Today it's very hard for me to face menopause when I will lose going to mikvah because I will lose that intensity of longing. Mikvah makes me recognize the process of aging, the fears that I face, the changes that are coming.

Exhibition Schedule:

Jewish Community Center of Houston
Houston, Texas
November-December, 2001

Galveston Arts Center *(in conjunction with Fotofest 2002)*
Galveston, Texas
February-March, 2002

Spertus Museum, Spertus Institute of Jewish Studies
Chicago, Illinois
April-October, 2002

Janice Charach Epstein Gallery
West Bloomfield, Michigan
November-December, 2002

Institute of Texan Cultures
San Antonio, Texas
March-April, 2003

The Women's Museum: An Institute for the Future
Dallas, Texas
April-May, 2003

Singer Gallery of The Mizel Center for Arts and Culture
Denver, Colorado
Summer 2003

Hebrew Union College-Jewish Institute of Religion Museum
New York City
Spring 2004

For additional venues, please visit
www.MikvahProject.com

Janice Rubin
Pnotographer

Janice Rubin is a Houston-based photographer and teacher. Originally from Fort Worth, she studied photography at Rice University from 1973-1977. Her work has been exhibited internationally. Her photographs are included in the permanent collection of the Museum of Fine Arts, Houston, as well as many private collections. She was the recipient of the National Endowment for the Arts Fellowship for her participation in the travelling exhibit "The Ties that Bind: Photographers Look At The American Family." Since 1976, her work has appeared in publications in the United States and Europe including *Smithsonian, Newsweek, Town and Country, Fortune, Rolling Stone,* and the *New York Times*. Her 1987 exhibition, "Survival of the Spirit: Jewish Lives in the Soviet Union" toured seventeen cities in the North America. She is also a musician and performing artist, speciallizing in Yiddish folk music. In 1995, she released her recording, "Feels Like Family" on the Heymish Music label.

Leah Lax
Writer

Leah Lax is a writer, teacher, and mother of seven children. She holds a Bachelor of Fine Arts in Art History from the University of Texas, and is currently an MFA candidate in the University of Houston Creative Writing Program. She has conducted numerous seminars for teachers and has been a lecturer for Jewish educational groups in synagogues and adult educational programs. Leah has also been a guest lecturer for the Houston Independent School District and the Texas Institute for Speech and Hearing to speak about language development and children with special needs. As a free-lance writer, she was mentored by novelists Rosellen Brown and Daniel Stern.

Charles Wiese
Creative Consultant

Charles Wiese was born in Detroit, Michigan. He is the creative consultant for the Mikvah Project, responsible for exhibition design, graphic design, web design, and printing of the project. He spent twelve years in research science and engineering before earning his MFA in photography and computer imagery from the University of Houston. Charles is a recipient of a Cultural Arts Council of Houston/Harris County 1995 Visual Artist Award, a Core Fellowship Artist-in-Residence at the Museum of Fine Arts/Houston, and is a fellow of the American Photography Institute at NYU/Tisch School of Art. He is an exhibiting artist and has taught at the University of Houston and Rice University and operates Studio Polygonia in Houston. He is married to Janice Rubin.